Poems on Civility

Poems on Civility

It Starts with You and Depends on You

S T KIMBROUGH, JR.

Foreword by Charles Amjad-Ali

RESOURCE *Publications* · Eugene, Oregon

POEMS ON CIVILITY
It Begins with You and Depends on You

Resource Publications
An Imprint of Wipf and Stock Publishers
199 W. 8th Ave., Suite 3
Eugene, OR 97401

www.wipfandstock.com

PAPERBACK ISBN: 979-8-3852-5115-5
HARDCOVER ISBN: 979-8-3852-5116-2
EBOOK ISBN: 979-8-3852-5117-9

Contents

CONTENTS

Foreword

Give us the will, strength to resist
that somehow justice can persist.[1]

If we see then equality
     as justice won for all,
for all the human family;
     it's human protocol.[2]

S T, IN THIS latest collection entitled *Poems on Civility: It Starts with You and Depends on You,* has once again given us profound insights and guidance of how we morally navigate the contemporary darkness. These seemingly small sparks of light act as beacons for traversing the murky path we are on today. He attempts to articulate the contemporary ways we live and participate in cultural, social, and civic communities in the US, and also in the world. We are witnessing the systematic dismantling of the socio-political order we have lived with since the aftermath of the Second World War. S T challenges us to look afresh at our operational ethical norms using poetic language to articulate both the sources of our disease as well as our hopes. He also names the contemporary difficulties which are directly aiding and abetting the anti-democratic forces and the intense opposition to the rights regimes that have been in place since the Second World War and have served for the good of society across the world.

In this darkness we must search even for small sparks of light for such aid—the *klein Funklein* which German mystic Meister

---

1. Poem #20, It Can't be So.
2. Poem #22, Equality.

Eckhart mentioned. S T has caught and given us a deep glimpse into the moral abyss we face as a human community, not just here in the USA but also around the world. All that we have tried to achieve through philosophy, religion, spirituality, mysticism, et al., is being treated as worthless remnants of bygone times, having no contemporary cultural, social, or political value. He has borne witness to the deep unsettling and frightening experience that we are going through, where everything that is good is being negated, belittled, and denied as having no purpose in human just, harmonious, and peaceful dwelling. We are indeed facing a deep, deep crisis of meaning and values! It appears to be an unstoppable descent into the state of darkness and/or despair, as Nietzsche describes in his book *Beyond Good and Evil*.[3] Nietzsche was deeply concerned with power and its impact when such power is unchecked and exerts itself upon the world. This has found a more poetic and imaginative portrayal by S T in this collection. It is not only will to power, it is will to power over all that is good, just, peaceful, and sustainable. This is a monarchical and dictatorial way of forcing one's will on the people, and it is destroying the very concept of the Republic (the will of the people) through oligarchic imposition and exercise of power. We are once again adopting a way of being which we thought we had got rid of in 1775/6—a monarchical non-democratic will to power.

S T reminds us that we now need to reclaim the spirit of resistance which began in the Old North Church in Boston in 1775, which ultimately led to the formation of the first modern Constitutional Republic in 1789, which removed the tyranny of single monarchical rule and oligarchies of power. It is critical to acknowledge that this new dark monarchical, oligarchic rule is ironically itself a product of the "democratic process." We are reminded again with Nietzsche that when you stare into the abyss—the abyss stares back at you.

In the face of this blight, S T not only points to the sources of this moral trauma, he also evokes principles which are foundational and provide us hope for more just, participatory, and

---

3. *Beyond Good and Evil*, translated by Walter Kaufmann, 1966; reprinted by Vintage Books, 1989, and as part of *Basic Writings of Nietzsche*, 1992.

sustainable social communities. He once again demonstrates how the language of poetry is different from conventional language use because it has imaginative and aesthetic patterns that are not easily accessible through normal viewing. He uses concepts, metaphors, synecdoche, and icons to stretch our imagination, and these poetic expressions point us to a different kind of knowledge and the difference between "knowing" and "being wise." What makes poetry so much more potent than flat scientific knowing is that aesthetics encompasses knowledge of human creativity, culture, and civilization, as it evokes our sensory perceptions and values both for assessment as well as critique of that which violates them. He directs us to the awareness of the plight of the poor, the wretched, the maligned, and the disregarded from the perspective of a deep proclivity for egalitarian understanding based on the very act of God's human creation in God's own icon-image, cf. Genesis 1:26–30.

As I was reading this collection of highly moral, highly ethical, and highly compassionate poems with their advice, counsel, and indeed imperatives, I was moved to a deep sense and awareness of the level of trauma that we are experiencing and the lack of general goodwill that pervades society. At that point I was forcibly reminded of Heidegger's concept of the "simple notion of care." It is not simple; it is deeply layered and deeply significant. Caring cannot be wiped out by any fiat if human beings are to survive socially, ethically, morally, in the world we live in. For Heidegger care (*Sorge*) defines or describes the whole of his concept of *dasein*, or being there, for it defines the world we live in and what we can be with caring. This is best defined in his famous *Being and Time*[4] which also remains the theme that S T pursues in all his poems. Though we are limited by the world we live in, we also continue to be enticed by caring for a better world than the one we inherited and the one we live in now. Throughout this volume we see S T directing us towards such caring on different issues, from different perspectives; he asks us to care for our neighbor and the world and its future.

4. Martin Heidegger, *Being and Time*, 2008.

We should not get so busy in the busy-ness of life and the avoidance of the doing of the good that we forget the care we must take, because it depends on us and begins and ends with us. To take the classical Thomist argument, when we are towards the good we are towards God. Not only the divine of the created order but also the divine of the good and caring selves we must be. There are some brilliant insights, assessments, analysis, and critiques that S T plays with and argues for. This whole collection is a pronouncement of poetic imagination about these assessments and about paths to follow and seek in this darkened time. For indeed "in Christ God was reconciling the world to himself, not counting their trespasses against them, and entrusting the message of reconciliation to us. So we are ambassadors for Christ, since God is making his appeal through us; we entreat you on behalf of Christ, to be reconciled to God" (2 Corinthians 5:19–20, NRSV). This has a broader missiological imperative on all who are called after the one who was crucified and resurrected. We are now located between the despair of the Crucifix of Good Friday and the seeming appearance of the victory of the Roman imperial power and their Golgothas on the one side, and the hope and resurrection of Easter on the other. We can therefore loudly proclaim, "Where, O desth, is your victory? Where, O death, is your sting?" (1 Corinthians 15:55, NRSV). Clearly the cross is essential for our salvation, but it doesn't stop there—even the resurrected (dare I say transformed) Jesus continues to bear the marks of that cross and was ready to show these marks to all the skeptics who wanted to place their fingers in the holes in the hands and feet and their hand in his pierced side. This is our hope in the face of this pervasive darkness and drought of moral reasoning.

Rev. Prof. Dr. Charles Amjad-Ali
The Martin Luther King, Jr., Prof.
of Justice and Christian Community (Emeritus)
Director of Islamic Studies (Emeritus)
Luther Seminary
St. Paul, MN

Introduction

ALTHOUGH CIVILITY MAY SOMETIMES have been viewed as formal politeness and courtesy in one's speech and behavior, its meaning has become more complex in contemporary society. It certainly still has to do with how we speak and act, but these are overlaid with political and partisan meanings, and a variety of media and social media options. There is the question of civility in private life, civility in public life, and now civility in cyber life. Plato (b. ca. 428/427, d. ca. 348/347 BCE) advised and warned "The price good men pay for indifference to public affairs is to be ruled by evil men."[1] Similarly Ralph Waldo Emerson (1803–1882) emphasized that this remains a modern concern as well when he said, "One of the penalties for refusing to participate in politics, is that you end up being governed by your inferiors."[2]

Who has the right to determine values and attitudes? Who has the right to declare what is the truth? What is to be said of reason, understanding, kindness, treatment of others, strangers? How does one deal with private and public conflict fairly? Clearly from culture to culture, nation to nation, the nuances of civility may vary, even greatly.

One thing is certain: whatever the responses humans make that constitute aspects of civility anywhere in the world, it begins with human beings. They are the source of civility or the lack of it.

1. *Republic,* Book 1, 347c, Perseus Digital Library.
2. "Eloquence," in *Society and Solitude,* 1870.

xi

Where do we find that honesty
is not turned into falsity?

Where do we find that decency
does not become a malady?

The only place that these are found
is where goodwill and peace abound.

So human beings are the source
of all that makes these things a force,

a force for all that they should be,
a force for human dignity![3]

Most surely Plato and Socrates were men of deep concern for
civility, as their writings reflect. If one moves forward to seven-
teenth- and eighteenth-century Europe, particularly to England at
the time of the explorations that led to the establishment of colo-
nies on the North-American continent, the struggle for civility is
glaringly evident. Martin B. Becker addresses this struggle in his
interesting volume, *The Emergence of Civil Society in the Eighteenth
Century: A Privileged Moment in the History of England, Scotland,
and France.*[4] The social divide in society was distinct: tensions
between social solidarity and self-interest were apparent. There
were strong advocates of politeness, refinement, and manners, and
these aspects of so-called civility became a part of the vocabulary
of the intelligentsia. If one did not conform to these social mores,
one suffered severely and was viewed as someone of a lower class.

The bibliography on subjects related to civility in our time
is vast. Here are but a few examples:[5] *In Defense of Civility* by
James Calvin Davis (2010); *The Righteous Mind* by Jonathan Haidt
(2012); *This Land of Strangers* by Robert Hall (2012); *The Power of
Nice—How to Conquer the Business World with Kindness* by Linda
Kaplan Thaler and Robin Koval (2006); *The Age of American Un-
reason* by Susan Jacoby (2008); *The Lost Art of Listening* by Michael

3. See poem #2, Begins and Ends with You.
4. Indiana University, 1994.
5. See the Bibliographic Appendix for more bibliography.

P. Nichols (2009); *How Civility Works* by Keith J. Bybee (2016); *Creating a New Civility* by Joy Marsella (2020).

This book of poetry says nothing new about diverse types of civility, or lack of them, that has not been said before, however, it accentuates many emphases related to civility with words, phrases, images, metaphors, and similes that may help us to think more vividly and act more intentionally to create a more civil society. The four sections follow a progression: "Civility Starts with You," "Civility Depends on You," "Civility Must Be Discussed," and "Civility Must Be Done." Civility requires creative thinking and creative action.

Above all else, civility expects a just and equal regard for all human beings.

Being Human

Uncivil in uncivil time
   of anger and vile hate;
autocracy is in its prime
   more chaos to create.
Removal of the right to be
   a person with respect;
removal of one's dignity
   what else might one expect

from tyranny and anarchy,
   from exploitation, lies?
This is the way democracy
   both quickly, slowly dies.
Enrich the rich, take from the poor,
   stress inequality.
Without a doubt, it's very sure
   thus wins autocracy.

A human being is just that,
   yes, human's what I mean.
Extend to all a welcome mat;
   let nothing come between,

between respect and decency
   for every soul on earth,
regarding each one equally—
   our lives long, from our birth.

Has there ever been a society on earth where civility reigned, where everyone truly had equal rights and respect? Unfortunately there is no trace of such a society anywhere in the world.

All humankind is only freed
   when everyone has equal rights,
the rights for which we all must plead:
   the blacks, browns, yellows. reds, and whites.[6]

To recognize the postures and activities of autocrats and anarchists is not always easy at the outset of their takeover of power.

The anarchists have devious skill,
   to take your human rights away,
with evil intent every day;
   warped "justice" is a game they play.[7]

Recognition of wrong-directed activities of leaders is one thing, but civility must be thought through and discussed. There is always the tendency of autocrats and anarchists to take away the rights of free speech and discussion.

To hear opposing, honest views
   with open and clear minds,
and question not who'll win or lose
   helps find a truth that binds.
It is indeed a rarity
   that parties, who oppose
each other, listen carefully,
   to things others disclose.[8]

If the art of listening carefully to one another is lost, civility vanishes.

---

6. See poem #12, Closed or Open Doors?

7. See poem #13, An American's Plea.

8. See poem #28, Reconciliation.

The art of listening has taken on a new dimension with the question of cyber civility. The variety of cyber platforms provides multiple avenues for bullying, insult, and deception. This has resulted in embezzlement, suicides, murders, and a variety of gang violence and school shootings. Furthermore, with the advent of AI (Artificial Intelligence) there are new options to use sounds and images in ways that appear authentic, which often only advanced technology can distinguish as deception.

The variety of cyber financial and identity scams aimed at all ages in society reflects another severe violation of civility. The elderly are particularly susceptible to scam telephone calls from persons who pretend to be from civil and government agencies, other organizations, and businesses requesting personal information in order to solve a so-called major problem which urgently needs to be resolved. The acquisition of personal identity information has become the prime target of many of these illegal efforts.

The human mind has an amazing capacity to deceive or to discern the truth. Both transpire through human intent. One is not by nature deceptive or truthful. How the mind is conditioned and taught to think is vital to civility, or lack of it.

> But minds can be deceived, that's clear,
>   by falsity and lies.
> What's false may then as truth appear,
>   and truth most surely dies.
> Still minds have the capacity
>   to seek the truth through facts.
> A sign of keen sagacity:
>   based on the facts, one acts.[9]

To take the attitudes that "whatever will be, will be," or "who am I to do anything about the lack of civility?" leads to apathy, inaction, and sometimes tragedy and disaster. Wherever dictators reign—

---

9. See poem #32, A Nurtured Mind.

Somehow resistance will arise,
    at least so hist'ry tells.
Injustices will demonize,
    and opposition swells.
   . . .
Sometimes there's violence, bloodshed;
    sometimes reason will reign,
when leaders are by justice led,
    which can the peace sustain.[10]

The poems throughout this volume avow—

There is but one humanity,
    one people and one humankind.
So let us pray for sanity
    that harmony one people find.[11]

S T Kimbrough, Jr.

10. See poem #48, Whence All Nations?
11. See poem #50, To Be Humane.

Section 1: Civility Starts with You

1. It Starts with You

The willingness to care for those
    who're homeless, poor, afflicted, weak,
a depth of human posture shows,
    that life's more than what egos seek.

To see the homeless as your friends,
    just ask: "Have this you tried to do?"
Would you think to share dividends
    with those who don't dress, think like you?

How personal to share a meal
    with fam'ly, friends, with those you know.
Does eating with the poor appeal
    or would you such a meal forgo?

To do the things you advocate
    will open up the human heart,
and can a caring world create,
    but in each person it must start.

2. Begins and Ends with You

Where do we find the common sense
that's not turned into bold nonsense?

Where do we find that honesty
is not turned into falsity?

Where do we find that decency
does not become a malady?

The only place that these are found
is where goodwill and peace abound.

So human beings are the source
of all that makes these things a force,

a force for all that they should be,
a force for human dignity!

3. Personal Worth

If prized for worth for being me,
though many my worth may not see,
   can reason explain why?
Self-centeredness may well reveal
why others' worth has no appeal:
   to care, some do not try.

Though human worth's no rarity,
the fact is we need parity
   to challenge all our minds.
We need a sense of common good
in every city, neighborhood,
   that worth in each one finds.

4. The Mirror

What did you see in the mirror
    each time you looked and stared?
Did you think as you got nearer—
    that through the years you'd fared?

You looked in at age twenty-two,
    your hair was full and brown.
At fifty-two what would you do?
    You saw gray all around.

At sixty-five, when you retired,
    you looked, your clothes didn't fit.
You weren't the weight that you desired;
    those sweets you should have quit.

At seventy you were so glad
    that you were still alive.
You looked and thought, "The looks I had
    back then I can't revive."

5. Truth and Lies

Try to legitimize a lie,
it's then the truth appears to die.
But truth can rise up from the grave
from gross dishonesty to save.
A lie endures for just a while,
but truth will go the extra mile.
The liars think that they have won,
but truth will keep them on the run.
A lie has great fragility,
but truth has durability.
Though lies will leave one all alone,
the truth will never one disown.

6. Can Humans Change?

Wherever human beings live,
    creating conflict and discord,
it's rarely that one hears "forgive,"
    forgiveness they cannot afford.

As greedy self-appeasement grows,
    self-satisfaction and self-gain
force social justice to new lows
    and create economic pain.

Equality's a rarity
    where self-concern rules and prevails,
and lost is gen'rous charity,
    and care for others sadly fails.

No race, no nation has the right
    to force some people to be poor,
to utilize wealth, pow'r, and might
    to make their poverty secure.

7. Deep Breaths

"Just take a deep breath," you have heard.
   Does this mean just relax?
Or is this a more serious word,
   requiring serious facts?

Without deep breath life slips away;
   we need it to survive.
With deep breath we begin each day,
   deep breaths keep us alive.

Give thanks for deep breaths every day,
   for each one that you take.
Give thanks for each one while you may;
   just take them for your sake!

8. Hands

I lift my hands to help someone,
    someone who has no hands.
I'm humble as the deed's begun;
    I ask, "Do you have plans?"
I mean, "Do you need help today?"
    "I need help with my meals."
"My aide," she said, "was called away,
    "I'm by myself, how strange it feels."

I use my hands and never ask,
    What if they were not there?
I have no idea of the task
    to live without the pair
of hands I've had since I was born;
    they've helped me to eat food
and put my clothes on every morn:
    they've often changed my mood.

Yes, we depend upon our hands
    so much more than we think.
Whatever are the day's demands,
    hands are a vital link.
They simply do the task at hand
    and do not question why.
The hands are truly something grand,
    and rarely are they shy.

9. Aware?

Another day has come and gone.
How can this be? It was just dawn.
A noonday luncheon passed so fast.
Why can't the noon times longer last?
An afternoon nap came and went,
it seemed as though no time was spent.
The evening's come, I'm in a fix;
I wonder, is time playing tricks?
And now the shades of night close in,
but did this day not just begin?
Have I no deed of kindness done?
It's time now for the setting sun.

10. Don't Wait

Most often as I go my way—
    I make my plans quite carefully.
At other times perhaps I stray
    with plans ignored quite carelessly.

Sometimes I may not have a plan
    and many options cannot find.
And then, I wonder if I can
    pursue ones that may come to mind.

If opportunity I seek,
    I must not wait till it finds me.
This may indeed make options bleak.
    Proceed with bold sincerity.

If opportunity I make,
    it may transpire through intellect,
or through my skills, hence I partake
    of wisdom which makes circumspect.

Don't wait for things to come to you.
    How quickly they can pass you by.
Your options then perhaps are few,
    with lethargy the reason why!

Yet do not be too hasty, friend,
    the circumspection that you gain
let it then serve you to the end;
    then wisdom to discern will reign.

11. Human Potential

If helpful hands the world could change,
might helpful thoughts wrongs then exchange
injustice for goodwill, kind deeds,
which focus on the human needs
that prejudice and war exclude,
which hope deny with certitude?
The human will one must awake
to think and live for others' sake.
But must one's own needs not come first,
before another's hunger, thirst?
How difficult it is to live
and think first, "What have I to give
to those who daily live without?"
Can I the answer carry out?
I know I need to think this through;
it's not a simple thing to do!

Section 2: Civility Depends on You

12. Closed or Open Doors?

Do closed doors offend humankind?
    They do, if they're to keep you out.
That is, if they're closed and you find
    the reason's prejudice, no doubt.

When doors of opportunity
    are closed because of race or creed,
or gender, all humanity
    is threatened, and it can't be freed.

All humankind is only freed
    when everyone has equal rights,
the rights for which we all must plead:
    the blacks, browns, yellows, reds, and whites.

The open doors have this to say,
    "You're welcome here, yes everyone."
"We welcome all," is no cliché.
    It's thus equality's begun.

13. An American's Plea

Division and polarity
now threaten our civility,
as well as our democracy.
Greed, power, and dishonesty,
revenge and vile hostility,
misogyny, vulgarity,
indecent immorality,
are laced with bold brutality.
To those who choose not to conform,
then violence becomes the norm
without the chance wrong to reform?
Americans, have you no will
such anarchy to stop, to still?
The anarchists have devious skill,
to take your human rights away,
with evil intent every day;
warped "justice" is a game they play.
Their interest is in self alone,
and selfishness they now enthrone
for which they never will atone.
America is on the brink
into the worst chaos to sink,
if leaders just of self will think.
Elect a president who'll call
the people to resist cabal:
be all for one and one for all.

14. The Politicians' Game

The politicians' game is "blame,"
  which nullifies civility.
They utter an opponent's name,
  displaying their hostility.

They must attack one's character;
  it matters not if it is true.
They play the role, disparager;
  accuse, accuse, that's what they do!

Promoting that for which one stands
  is noble, if it seeks the good,
but some serve self with greedy hands,
  and never act the way they should.

If politicians learned to care,
  and people thought their views were heard,
perhaps respect they'd learn to share,
  and governing wouldn't be absurd.

15. Apathy vs. Democracy

This is no time for apathy
when threats made to democracy
are made by those thirsting for pow'r
with their deception hour by hour.

World history is filled with those
who've tried for common good to pose,
but had one single goal in mind;
to keep all to their will confined.

This has brought many nations doom
where poverty and illness loom
and evil forces decades last;
where peoples can't forget their past.

Where there's no sense of unity,
some seize the opportunity
as dictators to rise,
for egotistic power's the prize.

There must be those with strength to fight
against a dictator's own might.
Those, who'll oppose unto the end
someone who's not the people's friend.

Americans have power to vote;
refuse it and, oh my, take note:
your freedom, dignity are lost.
Refuse to vote and that's the cost.

The ballot box is there for those,
who dictatorship will oppose.
So, exercise your right to vote:
democracy and peace promote!

From a John Wesley letter to Thomas Maxfield, November 2, 1762:

"But what I most of all dislike is your *littleness of love* to your brethren, to your own society: your want of *union of heart* with them and 'bowels of mercies'[1] toward them; your want of *meekness, gentleness, long-suffering*, your 'impatience of contradiction';[2] your counting every man your enemy that reproves or admonishes you in love; your *bigotry* and *narrowness* of spirit, loving in a manner only those that love *you*; your *censoriousness*, proneness to *think hardly* of all who do not exactly agree with you: in one word, your *divisive spirit*."[3]

16. Lack of Unity

Your lack of unison and love,
placing yourselves so far above
the gospel's plea for unity,
shows you prefer to disagree.

You've narrowness and bigotry
by which you judge each enemy.
You love those who say they love you;
you think the gospel's for a few,

the few who see it as they do.
To truth they've found the hidden clue:
it must be viewed through their own eyes,
for other views they will despise.

1. Colossians 3:12.
2. Cf. Hebrews 12:3.
3. See *Bicentennial Edition of John Wesley's Works*, 27:308.

Amos 5:14–15, 24: "Seek good and not evil, that you may live; and so the Lord, the God of hosts, will be with you, just as you have said. Hate evil and love good, and establish justice in the gate; it may be that the Lord, the God of hosts, will be gracious to the remnant of Joseph. . . . But let justice roll down like waters, and righteousness like an ever-flowing stream." (NRSV)

17. Dead or Living Hope?

"Seek good, and not evil, and live,
    establish justice in the gate."
These are the things each has to give,
    which evil, hatred can abate.

All hope of Amos' earnest plea
    is shattered by death bombs and guns.
Where is there justice one can see?
    Israel acts like Attila's Huns.

Is Amos' hope forever lost
    where violence and evil reign?
Where victors care not what's the cost
    of endless death-inflicted pain.

Still Amos cries, "Let justice roll,
    roll down like waters, flowing streams;"
let evil no more take its toll,
    fulfilling ancient prophets' dreams.

18. A Wish for All

Some hope a wish can be fulfilled
    but others don't hope so;
they know a wish cannot be willed,
    yet wishes grow and grow.

Do you recall a birthday cake
    with candles that were bright?
All wondered what wish you would make,
    which you would not recite.

You made a wish, blew candles out
    and thought, Will it come true?
You knew for sure, without a doubt,
    the wish was just for you.

Some children never wishes make;
    they live in such despair.
They've never had a birthday cake.
    It's time for us to care.

19. Faith-Ego

There is a charm in being you,
a Christian, Muslim, or a Jew.
All children might think this were true,
if they weren't taught it is not so,
by elders who think that they know
that other folks are far below
their station and ethnicity,
their faith, religiosity,
and those who live in poverty.
Are Muslims better than the Jews?
Are Christians better when they choose
to follow Jesus? Who will lose?
Do Jews think they're the chosen few
and other faiths don't have a clue?
If so, what are these faiths to do?
Shed faith-ego and humble be,
and value everyone you see.
and live love's creativity.
If God is love, as we should learn,
then no one's bound this love to earn,
so ev'ry heart to love should turn.

20. It Can't Be So!

Does no one in the USA
have strength and will to cast away
the ego-centered policies
which threaten all democracies:
self-serving int'rests that ignore
the weak, the poor, and wealth adore?

"Give me your tired, your poor, your weak!"
Our forebears said; were they too meek?
In a strong nation we must change,
no matter if it may seem strange.
Forget the poor, honor the strong
and hope the people go along.

A nation born by immigrants
now has a leader who just rants!
He cannot stop his vicious tongue
against the sick, the old, and young.
Surrounds himself with servants all
who follow every beck and call.

When will it end? We do not know.
Each day we say, "It can't be so."
The right to think, and speak, and do,
will they be lost, all freedoms too?
Give us the will, strength to resist,
that somehow justice can persist.

21. Practice What You Preach

How often it is simply said,
   "Just practice what you preach,"
much easier to say instead—
   "It's just a form of speech."
We say it, then decide instead,
   to do what comes to mind,
which means sometimes we lose our head
   and leave our sense behind.

We leave ourselves so far behind
   the truth we may hold dear.
To think of others and be kind
   we sacrifice to fear,
the fear that our way's not the way
   things always will be done.
We fight to have things done today
   our way, the battle's won.

But truth does not permit that we
   hold on to our own way
and everything quite selfishly
   then leave in disarray.
With hope go on, devoid of fear,
   grant dignity, respect
for every person far and near,
   so prejudice is checked.

Section 3: Civility Must Be Discussed

22. Equality

If people cannot live to care
    for family, neighbors, friends,
for those whose presence they can't bear,
    their lives have senseless ends.

The only way lives can have worth:
    see worth in everyone,
in every nation of the earth;
    equality is won.

Equality alone is just!
    Without equality
there never can be mutual trust
    throughout humanity.

But mutual trust carries a cost,
    the cost of sacrifice:
when dominance of self is lost,
    it is a worthy price.

If we see then equality
    as justice won for all,
for all the human family;
    it's human protocol.

23. Despair or Care

There's been no time without despair,
no time without the need for care.
There is despair that nature brings,
despair that from disasters springs:
a home destroyed by hurricanes,
a life that's lost by flooding rains.
But there's despair humans create
by filling hearts and minds with hate:
despair of an abusive tongue
that ruins the lives of old and young;
despair that politicians make
who legislate for ego's sake;
despair of nations going to war,
where families mourn death's daily score.
Despair of friendships that we lose,
because we wrong decisions choose.
What hope can there be for repair
of deep, deep wounds made by despair?
A sense of caring must arise
in us until we others prize.
For this, there is no substitute:
when we don't care, we're destitute!
If we would change lives of despair
to ones that show how much we care,
then act with caring love, forgive,
and others may choose thus to live.

24. Difference

The diff'rence can mean many things,
     perhaps things aren't at all alike.
From diff'rence often contrast springs:
     from country road to a turnpike.

The difference is often good,
     if it helps us make the best choice;
bad when we don't act as we should:
     we don't like someone's diff'rent voice.

"They're very diff'rent," some may say,
     Republican or Democrat.
"They think and speak a diff'rent way.
     How can a person think like that?"

And what of diff'rent colored skin,
     black, yellow, white, or red, and brown?
Is that the way we know our kin?
     Should diff'rent colors cause a frown?

The diff'rent colors of spring flow'rs
     across a meadow in the spring,
a view we cherish for long hours;
     creation's gift and offering.

An off'ring to all humankind,
     to all creation's vast array
of diff'rences for every mind
     to grasp and cherish day by day.

25. Humility

The sign of Christianity:
for certain is humility.
Macarius does this advise,
and thus Macarius is wise.
If you are humble, you don't know.
Humility you cannot show,
except if you are unaware.
It's thus humility you share.
It's said, "One needs a humble mind."
It's said, "A humble person's kind."
It's said, "One needs a humble heart;"
a humble heart you can't impart.
"How humble I am," do not say,
for pride will block the humble way.
Humility's a mystery.
and yet it's a reality.

26. Infinity

Who can define infinity?
It's endless as eternity.
Infinity's a mystery;
we cannot read its history.
In math it is indeed well known;
its science value's grown and grown.
Infinity—endless, unbound;
infinity's never been found.
Its symbol's horizontal eight,
and yet its meaning we await.
Infinity's mathematical;
infinity is physical;
it's also metaphysical.
Infinity's not showable;
will it someday be knowable?

27. Reality?

What are sheep with no shepherd?
    What are shepherds with no sheep?
If spotless were a leopard,
    has one's reason gone to sleep?

What if what we think is not
    the way things are known to be?
Is reality then fraught
    with that which we do not see?

Hard, cold facts, oft hard to find,
    sometimes are before our eyes.
Don't speculate, don't be blind:
    choose the facts instead of lies.

28. Reconciliation

To reconcile one needs consent
    of those locked in conflict,
to quell the anger some foment
    and turmoil they predict.

To hear opposing, honest views
    with open and clear minds,
and question not who'll win or lose
    helps find a truth that binds.

It is indeed a rarity
    that parties, who oppose
each other, listen carefully,
    to things others disclose.

If reconciliation's found,
    where it's expected least,
amelioration may be found,
    in north, south, west, and east.

29. Time

Time passes by, often unknown,
quite unaware time may have flown.
It may pass by unknown to me
for time's a unique mystery.
Though it can be very exact,
and our attention may attract;
it's there and suddenly it's gone.
In spite of time, we carry on.

30. Serenity

Serenity means calm repose
to those who peaceful thoughts compose.
It ushers in tranquility,
which gives one the facility
to rest, to think, to be at peace,
ev'n though one's anxiousness increase.
Serenity is hard to learn,
if one for calmness does not yearn.
Serenity: just stop and hear,
for quietness will then appear.
Serenity's something we feel;
we sense serenity is real.
If you have ever been serene,
you know exactly what I mean.

31. So What!

There is no reason, reason knows
why evil, evil always shows
there is no sensibility
in making evil seem to be
the only recourse humans find
to treat the evils of mankind.
For greed there is but one response:
more greed that wreaks of nonchalance.
Just take and take and then take more,
no matter that the poor implore—
"I'm hungry, sick, and very weak."
The rich care not their future's bleak.
Can one replace rapacity
with caring love's capacity?
If not, then greedy tyrants' rule
will make of everyone a fool.

32. A Nurtured Mind

Each day if sunlight had the power
    to activate the mind,
the way it activates a flower,
    our thoughts might be refined.
They'd flourish, bloom, and daily grow
    until our minds would be
prepared to grasp what they don't know
    and better learn to see.

A flow'r draws strength one cannot see
    from sunlight and the soil.
Our minds draw strength, sagacity
    from study, wisdom, toil.
Our minds draw strength we cannot see,
    like flowers from sunlight, earth.
Take care that they well nurtured be;
    it's then they can have worth.

Sunlight's the key energy source
    for plants no matter where.
The sunlight keeps plants on the course
    of life, a course they share.
It's thus plants will produce their food;
    hence they survive and grow.
Our minds grow for the ill or good
    from all we learn and know.

But minds can be deceived, that's clear,
    by falsity and lies.
What's false may then as truth appear,
    and truth most surely dies.

Still minds have the capacity
    to seek the truth through facts.
A sign of keen sagacity:
    based on the facts, one acts.

33. That Word "Immigrant"

Is "immigrant" an evil word?
Not so, that would be too absurd.
For in the USA today
we're immigrants all, one must say,
except for native peoples all,
who immigrants made sure would fall.
There is no one superior race,
which leaves of no one else a trace.
Although this often has been tried,
success has always been denied.
Oppression leads to just one fate:
despair and anger, and gross hate.
And hate's an omen of the fall
of those who think they'll misuse all.
The fate in human history,
when rulers create misery,
oppress the citizens and steal
their livelihoods with no appeal,
and do away with honesty,
they create a gross travesty.
And thus, oppressed folk surely rise.
This is by no means a surprise.
They then defeat oppressors all,
who slowly, quickly then will fall.

34. Where Have They Gone?

Have decency and honesty
    just vanished with the wind,
like vicious storms that rapidly
    upon the world descend?

A view of people that's humane
    in leaders quickly dies;
their speech, their actions so profane:
    democracy's demise.

Examples for a child they're not
    of what one wants to be.
But rather they're an awful blot
    on our land's history.

These are such very simple words,
    why should one write them down?
They'll vanish like the flight of birds
    since greed has come to town.

35. A Solitary Place

A solitary place I sought
    to gather thoughts and then to rest.
I was not weary or distraught
    and did not sense I was distressed.

It's good to seek a quiet place
    before it's something that you need.
If quietly your thoughts you'll trace,
    it's doubtful you'll to stress accede.

Especially thoughts you avoid,
    don't shelter them from all critique,
or else by them you'll be annoyed;
    you'll find results could be quite bleak.

So turn aside to rest, reflect,
    examine, test the things you think.
And carefully those thoughts reject,
    which you cannot with sane thought link.

36. To Think

Think carefully, think sensibly,
intelligently, thoughtfully.
Think earnestly, think prayerfully,
think winsomely, think artfully.
There are so many ways to think.
Words, images provide a link;
imagination fills the void
when all our powers are employed.

Section 4: Civility Must Be Practiced

37. The Lost Art of Listening

Demise of civil discourse haunts
    what's left of our democracy.
Division like an illness taunts
    what's left of human sanity.

Where listening is a long-lost art
    and agitation, rancor rage,
there's no place for the human heart
    and no room for a truthful sage.

Polarity feeds anarchy
    where power lust consumes the free
and takes away all liberty;
    free thought is a non-entity.

If serious listening can't return
    so people one another hear,
like Nero's Rome nations will burn,
    and history's lessons disappear.

38. Democracy?

Democracy, some would allege,
now teeters on destruction's edge.

Political ascendancy
now crushes human decency.

A president's carnality,
should it be a normality?

A vulgar, crass banality,
now praises illegality.

There's no sense of morality,
which leads to criminality.

Can we not face reality
and banish such rascality!

39. Out of Control

I'm living in a land that's free,
    at least that's what I'm told.
But guns used in a killing spree
    shows they are not controlled.

A child is lost, a mother, son,
    a drive-by shooting's fate.
Gun-lobbyists again have won,
    and gun shops celebrate.

"The problem is by no means guns;
    it's simply their misuse."
It's thus the explanation runs:
    a pitiful excuse!

Excuse that lets school children die,
    which happens every year.
And legislators wonder why
    school-families live in fear.

40. Be Strong or Weak?

Strength and weakness fill our days.
Strength we hope we'll have always;
weakness we hope's just a phase.
Strength how happily we praise;
weakness we must reappraise.
Strength may help us change our ways.
Strength and weakness, what contrast!
Can our strength weakness outlast?

41. To Sleep

What matters most when you're awake?
For some to wake's too much to take.
Some will awake in every clime,
but others wake for one last time,
We go to sleep, think we'll awake
and take for granted there's no break
in sleeping's cycle night by night,
when sunlight bows to bright moonlight.
But some folk work when others sleep,
and different sleeping hours keep.
Around the world, around the clock
from New York to Far East's Bangkok,
all people of all nations sleep
and from it rest and strength will reap.
When they awake, they all should think
that common habits are a link
to help them see a human bond
that changes how they then respond
to one another every day,
by being kind in every way.

42. To Wait

To wait, the vocation of all;
to wait, you must wait for a call.
To wait is boring, wrong to some;
to wait, some will think it's quite dumb.
To wait, you may find out what's true.
To wait, you may learn what to do.
To wait, can often make hearts sing;
to wait's the most important thing.
To wait, to wait many forget.
To wait, to wait makes some folks fret.

43. Try Love

Love, love's the only force to heal
divisions humans make so real.
Misunderstandings, disbelief
lead many lovers into grief.

They do not want to be a part
of matters dealing with the heart.
Love opens hearts, creates desire
to care and be a unifier.

Try love, the healing force that's real.
Try love, which closed hearts will unseal.
An open heart will find a way
to create trust, not lead astray.

44. Make Music

A day that's filled with music brings
a joy through which one's spirit sings.
A routine, daily atmosphere
transforms to unexpected cheer.
It turns bleak darkness into light,
and saddened moments soon take flight.
When mother touched piano keys,
it was as though the freshest breeze
had wafted through the music room,
to lift all care and banish gloom.
When father hit a strong high note,
the trembling windows seemed to float.
With instruments or sounds of song,
the music carries us along
mysterious ways, and lifts the soul
in life and death, from pole to pole.
If hip hop, or its rock and roll,
a church hymn or a barcarole,
in music there is insight, power
to make the human spirit flower.

45. The Right to Vote

"The right to vote," so I was told,
by my grandpa when he was old,
"is one of our most precious rights
for which each honest person fights."
So many died that we might vote;
it's not a casual anecdote.
They gave their lives so everyone
could choose how each election's won.
If you don't vote, then you defy
all those who for your right did die.
No citizen should be denied
this right for whom so many died.

46. Remembering Those Who've Passed

When bleeds the heart for those who've passed,
    their talent, personality,
one knows though bodies do not last,
    that talents, love, sincerity
for generations can live on,
    perhaps ev'n longer can endure:
from stories, knowledge, wisdom's drawn,
    of this we can be very sure.

But knowledge needs an advocate,
    ideas, stories, words as well.
How can they minds, hearts captivate?
    This comes not from a wishing well.
What makes our knowledge, gifts survive?
    Mere memory cannot suffice.
Through diligence and love they thrive—
    from ancient Greece comes this advice.

On interaction much depends,
    how human beings interact:
to others kindness each one lends,
    makes dignity a human fact;
makes culture, knowledge one's close friends,
    to colleagues' progress adds one's praise.
On neighbor love so much depends
    thus lived, one has rewarding days.

47. Whence Democracy?

Reflection, intellect, and sense
are orphans without recompense,
when facts and truth are both denied
and common sense likewise defied.
Disinformation's now a cult,
"Ignore the truth," its sad result.
Its foll'wers trust Trump's specious lies
and seek democracy's demise.
The future only holds the key
for those who want democracy
to triumph o'er subversive acts
by seeking truth that's based on facts.

48. Whence All Nations?

Whenever there is discontent
  among the peoples of a land,
quite often some will have a bent
  toward taking pow'r in hand.
At first it seems for common good
  they want to assume power,
but soon one wonders if they should,
  as leadership grows dour.

Somehow the sense that they control
  consumes their ego strain,
and at their mercy is each soul
  who's under their domain.
Somehow resistance will arise,
  at least so hist'ry tells.
Injustices will demonize
  and opposition swells.

Sometimes there's violence, bloodshed,
  sometimes reason will reign,
when leaders are by justice led,
  which can the peace sustain.
A land at peace, on justice built,
  can guide its people on
to harmony, absent of guilt,
  and enmity is gone.

But such a vision courage needs
  among a nation's throng
to follow just words with just deeds,
  distinguish right from wrong.

Sometimes the quest for justice seems
    so long and without ends;
and we surmise it's left to dreams,
    while on us it depends!

'

49. New Year Hope

A new year dawns with hope and fear,
the hope that there'll be cause to cheer,
    but fear it won't be so.
Some children laugh and happy play,
while others live from day to day
    and no affection know.

A new year's hope is ours to give,
when we seek justly so to live
    that others hope may find.
To live with others let us learn.
And let our hearts with kindness burn
    and share with love in mind.

The question's not—Will we find cheer
as we begin another year?
    Will someone else find cheer,
because we think of others first,
because in sharing we're well versed?
    Thus we'll begin the year!

50. To Be Humane

How can we learn to be humane?
  This knowledge we don't have at birth,
but as we grow, we need to gain
  the understanding of another's worth.

To be humane, yes, we can learn,
  but more than knowledge it must be.
It means we're willing to discern
  one's worth through sensitivity.

We're sensitive to each one's worth,
  a worth born of equality,
embracing every soul on earth
  and marked by inclusivity.

If this sounds like nice platitudes,
  which one may or may not accept,
perhaps we've ingrown attitudes
  and prejudice better not kept.

Each person born can be humane
  but there's a lifelong learning curve.
We're never perfect, hence we train
  till we to be humane have nerve.

We train to take all as they are—
  their language, culture, faith, and skin.
There's no one that we should debar;
  humaneness makes all people kin.

There is but one humanity,
  one people and one humankind.
So let us pray for sanity
  that harmony one people find.

51. Worthy Leadership?

The games that nation leaders play
    with lives for whom they've no concern
show how disdain is ego's way,
    and how they needs of others spurn.

The chasm in a leader's mind
    that ego easily creates,
will leave constituents behind
    to desperate and tragic fates.

Their rights to freedom, liberty,
    to speak their mind, and challenge wrong,
diminished to nonentity;
    they're made to feel they don't belong.

They don't belong with oligarchs,
    for wealth is not their major goal,
which once was said of Lenin, Marx,
    and yet they peoples' freedoms stole.

Where are the leaders whose first care
    is valuing humanity?
Who know equality all share,
    and aren't absorbed with vanity?

52. Equity or Inequity?

The word we know as equity
    is very rarely heard;
its opposite inequity
    by many is preferred.

The quality of being fair,
    fair-mindedness seems gone.
Some politicians even dare
    unfairness to lean on.

Inequitable is the word,
    that well describes today
behavior which fairness has blurred
    and ethical decay.

Will equity simply remain
    a word stock markets use?
It will, unless we few complain
    and words never abuse.

Remembering Bloody Sunday at the Edmund
Pettus Bridge in Selma, Alabama (1965)

53. Across the Bridge We're Marching Still

Across the bridge we're marching still,
    and Bloody Sundays multiply.
One searches for those with the will
    to fight for justice "by and by."
The poor, oppressed still sing the song,
    yes, "by and by when morning comes,"
but in their prayers they ask, "How long?"
    while justice to strong power succumbs.

Across the bridge we're marching still,
    as Selmas seem to multiply.
Have representatives no will
    to show they know the reasons why?
Why inhumaneness grows and grows,
    and scheming ways daily devised
keep voting rights at unjust lows
    for those who're by their skin despised.

Across the bridge we're marching still;
    who will decide to go along?
Refuse and we'll defeat the will
    and lifeblood of the freedom song.
We will not overcome some day,
    for deep in our hearts we believe:
there simply is no other way
    to triumph, but let others grieve.

Across the bridge we're marching still
    and history tells us, we are wrong,
if we refuse to heal the ill,
    which haunts all people centuries long—
to heal the prejudice and hate
    so often subtle in their ways.
It's time to act, lest it's too late
    and history sets our names ablaze!

54. Civility and the Cyber World

The cyber world, the internet,
    by which we now communicate,
embodies dangers, don't forget:
    identities can obviate.
The hackers, very cyber-wise,
    can take funds from our bank accounts,
and diverse scamming schemes devise
    to steal stocks, cash of vast amounts.

The scamming schemes seem without end,
    and minute after minute grow.
The cyber world we thought our friend
    reveals a most deceptive flow
of num'rous lies and non-stop schemes
    civility to violate,
by anyone who wants, it seems
    all civil good to confiscate.

Now AI comes upon the scene,
    and we don't know where we're to turn;
a voice is cloned, ways not foreseen
    merge images one can't discern
if they're authentic or they're fake.
    Where will wholesale deception end?
Somehow we must fight for truth's sake,
    whate'er the time that we must spend.

55. Social Media's Yoke

The social media abuse
    to some seems just a joke,
for bullying there's no excuse;
    for many it's a yoke:
a yoke so heavy it belies
    all goodness of intent,
until one's strength of spirit dies;
    desire for life is spent.

56. Cyber Threats

The threats that come from cyber space
    sometimes are realized.
They're often difficult to trace
    and cleverly disguised.

Perhaps they are an open threat
    which brazenly makes plain;
they may in minutes fear beget
    and even death or pain.

If cyber fear is weaponized
    with means of fear and hate,
with evil intent synchronized;
    it brings unwelcome fate.

Now nations shape new cyber spies
    in place of human minds,
and hacking substitutes its lies
    with these new cyber finds.

Bibliography on Civility

Backman, John. *Why Can't We Talk? Christian Wisdom on Dialogue as a Habit of the Heart.* Woodstock, VT: SkyLight Paths, 2013.

Bayer, Lewena. *The 30% Solution: How Civility at Work Increases Retention, Engagement and Profitability.* Melbourne, FL: Motivational, 2016.

Bechtle, Mike. *Dealing with the Elephant in the Room: Moving from Tough Conversations to Healthy Communications.* Grand Rapids, MI: Revell, 2017.

Berman, Lea and Jeremy Bernard. *Treating People Well: The Extraordinary Power of Civility at Work and in Life.* New York: Scribner, 2018.

Brands, H. W. *American Colossus: The Triumph of Capitalism 1865–1900.* New York: Doubleday, 2010.

Brooks, Arthur C. *Love Your Enemies: How Decent People Can Save America from a Culture of Contempt.* New York: Broadside Books, 2019.

Brooks, David. *The Road to Character.* New York: Random House, 2015.

Brown, Brené. *Braving the Wilderness: The Quest for True Belonging and the Courage to Stand Alone,* New York: Random House, 2017.

Bybee, Keith J. *How Civility Works.* Stanford: Stanford University, 2016.

Carter, Stephen. L *Civility: Manners, Morals, and the Etiquette of Democracy.* New York: Basic Books, 1998.

Clayton, Cornell W. and Richard Elgar, eds. *Civility and Democracy in America: A Reasonable Understanding.* Pullman, WA: Washington State University, 2012.

Davis, James Calvin. *In Defense of Civility: How Religion Can Unite America on Seven Moral Issues that Divide Us.* Louisville, KY: Westminster John Knox, 2010.

Davetian, Benet. *Civility: A Cultural History.* Toronto: University of Toronto, 2009.

Dobson, Bob. *American Story: A Lifetime Search for Ordinary People Doing Extraordinary Things.* New York: Plume/Penguin, 2014.

Edwards, Gavin. *Kindness and Wonder: Why Mister Rogers Matters Now More Than Ever.* New York: HarperCollins, 2019.

Eilperin, Juliet. *Fight Club Politics – How Partisanship is Poisoning the House of Representatives.* Lanham: Rowman & Littlefield, 2006.

Ellul, Jacques. *Meaning of the City.* Grand Rapids, Michigan: William B. Eerdmans, 1970.

———. *Money and Power.* Downers Grove, Illinois: Inter-Varsity, 1984.

Forni, P. M. *Choosing Civility: The Twenty-five Rules of Considerate Conduct.* New York: St. Martin's, 2002.

———. *The Thinking Life – How to Thrive in the Age of Distraction.* New York: St. Martin's, 2011.

Freshley, Craig. *The Wisdom of Group Decisions: 100 Principles and Practical Tips for Collaboration.* Brunswick, ME: Good Group Decisions, 2010.

Gerzon, Mark. *Leading Through Conflict – How Successful Leaders Transform Differences into Opportunities.* Boston, MA: Harvard Business School, 2006.

———. *The Reunited States of America: How We Can Bridge the Partisan Divide.* Oakland, CA: Berrett-Koehler Publishers, 2016.

Grumet, Jason. *City of Rivals: Restoring the Glorious Mess of American Democracy.* Guilford, CT: Lyons, 2014.

Gundersen, Adolf G. and Suzanne Goodney Lea. *Let's Talk Politics – Restoring Civility Through Exploratory Discussion.* [Scotts Valley, CA:] CreateSpace Independent, 2013.

Hacala, Sara. *Saving Civility – 52 Ways to Tame Rude, Crude & Attitude for a Polite Planet.* Woodstock, VT: SkyLight Paths, 2011.

Haidt, Jonathan. *The Righteous Mind: Why Good People Are Divided by Politics and Religion.* New York: Pantheon Books, 2012.

Hall, Robert. *This Land of Strangers: The Relationship Crisis That Imperils Home, Work, Politics, and Faith.* Austin, TX: Greenleaf Book Group, 2012.

Jacoby, Susan. *The Age of American Unreason.* New York: Pantheon Books, 2008.

Legothetis, Leon. *The Kindness Diaries: One Man's Quest to Ignite Goodwill and Transform Lives Around the World.* New York: Reader's Digest, 2015.

Marks, Stephen. *Confessions of a Political Hitman: My Secret Life of Scandal, Corruption, Hypocrisy and Dirty Attacks That Decide Who Gets Elected (and Who Doesn't).* Naperville, IL: Sourcebooks, 2007.

Marsella, Joy. *Creating a New Civility.* Akron, OH: University of Akron, 2020.

Matthews, David. *The Ecology of Democracy: Finding Ways to Have a Stronger Hand in Shaping Our Future.* Dayton, OH: Kettering Foundation, 2014.

Neisser, Philip T., and Jacob Hess. *You're Not as Crazy as I Thought: Conversations Between a Die-hard Liberal and a Devoted Conservative.* Washington, D.C.: Potomac Books, 2012.

Nichols, Michael P. *The Lost Art of Listening: How Learning to Listen Can Improve Relationships.* Second Edition. New York: Guilford, 2009.

Reich, Robert B. *The Common Good.* New York, NY: Alfred A. Knopf, 2018.

Sachs, Robert. *The Path of Civility: Perfecting the Lessons of a President By Applying the Wisdom of a Buddha.* [Winchester, Hampshire] United Kingdom: John Hunt, 2020.

Shriver, Jr. Donald W., Jr. *An Ethic for Enemies: Forgiveness in Politics.* New York: Oxford University, 1995.

Singular, Stephen. *The Uncivil War: The Rise of Hate, Violence, and Terrorism in America.* Beverly Hills: New Millenium, 2001.

Stone, Douglas, Bruce Patton, and Sheila Heen. *Difficult Conversations – How to Discuss What Matters Most.* New York, NY: Penguin, 1999.

Tannen, Deborah. *The Argument Culture: Stopping America's War of Words.* New York: Ballantine, 1998.

Thaler, Linda Kaplan and Robin Koval. *The Power of Nice: How to Conquer the Business World with Kindness.* New York: Crown Currency, 2006.

Truss, Lynne. *Talk to the Hand: The Utter Bloody Rudeness of the World Today or Six Reasons to Stay Home and Bolt the Door.* New York, NY: Gotham Books, 2005.

Walker, Cami. *29 Gifts: How a Month of Giving Can Change Your Life.* Boston, MA: Da Capo, 2009.

Weiland, Matt and Sean Wilsey, eds. *State by State: A Panoramic Portrait of America.* New York, NY: HarperCollins, 2008.

Woodward, Colin. *American Nations: A History of the Eleven Rival Regional Cultures of North America.* New York: Penguin, 2012.

Subject Index

SUBJECT INDEX

www.ingramcontent.com/pod-product-compliance
Lightning Source LLC
Chambersburg PA
CBHW052203090426
42741CB00010B/2382